Whispers of Artistry

In the shadows softly dance,
Colors mingle, chance romance.
Brushstrokes weave a tender tale,
As silence sings, the dreams set sail.

Glimmers caught in twilight's hue,
Canvas breathes, emotions true.
Each stroke whispers of delight,
Crafting visions into light.

Threads of Refined Grace

A tapestry of subtle hues,
Woven threads, passions fuse.
Delicate patterns softly sigh,
In harmony, they rise and fly.

Elegance in every fold,
Stories whispered, gently told.
Silken whispers in the breeze,
Crafting beauty, hearts at ease.

The Poise of Creation

Balanced forms in pure repose,
Mastery that gently flows.
Every line, a measure fine,
Breath of life in design divine.

Hands that sculpt with patient grace,
Inspiration finds its place.
Rhythms pulse with every beat,
Creation's dance, both bold and sweet.

Silhouettes in the Atelier

Figures cast in shades of night,
Mysteries held in the light.
In the studio, dreams come forth,
Artistry's true, vibrant worth.

Life portrayed in subtle shapes,
Reflections of the artist's drapes.
Silhouettes that move, that breathe,
Whispers of the soul beneath.

Poised in Passion

In shadows deep, the heart does race,
With every glance, a warm embrace.
The fire within, it starts to glow,
A whispered wish, a love to grow.

Through silent nights, the stars will weave,
A tapestry that none perceive.
Two souls entwined, in dreams they soar,
In poised passion, they yearn for more.

Whispers of Refined Artistry

Brush strokes dance on canvas bare,
Colors blend, a vibrant flare.
Each whisper tells a tale untold,
Of fleeting moments, brave and bold.

In every line, a story spins,
Subtle truths beneath the skin.
Crafted worlds where dreams take flight,
In refined artistry's pure light.

Chiseled Dreams in Gentle Light

Stone meets hand, the vision clear,
Chiseled dreams, the sculptor near.
Gentle light on edges play,
Revealing beauty in the clay.

With patience strong, each form defined,
Every curve, a dance aligned.
In marble's grace, the heart takes flight,
Crafting dreams in gentle light.

The Dance of Graceful Hands

Fingers glide like whispered breeze,
In harmony, they flow with ease.
With every move, a story spun,
The dance begins; the joy, a run.

In rhythm found, the world awakes,
Through graceful hands, the silence breaks.
A language clear, no words required,
In this embrace, pure hearts inspired.

Chiseled Dreams

In shadows deep, the chisel strikes,
Forming visions that break the night.
Carved from stone, a tale unfolds,
A whisper of dreams that time holds.

In silence kept, the heartbeats flow,
A dance of fate, where feelings grow.
Each stroke, a mark, of hope and fear,
In chiseled dreams, the path is clear.

Where Aesthetics Bloom

In gardens lush, where colors play,
Petals whisper secrets of the day.
Each hue a note, a song to share,
In fragrant air, lives beauty rare.

Amidst the light, the shadows sway,
Crafting magic, come what may.
In every glance, a story weaves,
Where aesthetics bloom, the soul believes.

Elegance Intertwined

In graceful lines, the moments dance,
Silken threads in a timeless trance.
Embracing light with tender grace,
Elegance woven in every space.

With whispered tones, the night descends,
As soft as dreams, where time suspends.
In every glance, a world aligned,
Reflections of what's intertwined.

The Fabric of Finesse

In layers rich, like stories told,
The fabric weaves through days of gold.
Stitched with care, in every seam,
A tapestry crafted from a dream.

With gentle hands, we shape and mold,
Each thread a heartbeat, brave and bold.
In patterns bright, our spirits dance,
In the fabric of finesse, we find our chance.

The Subtlety of Skilled Hands

In quiet corners, crafts take form,
With gentle strokes, the artisans warm.
Each curve and line, a story spun,
In every piece, a heart once won.

Tools dance lightly, in whispered grace,
Molding visions, giving space.
From humble start to finished gleam,
Skilled hands weave the fabric of dream.

Echoes of a Timeless Charm

Whispers linger in the twilight air,
Moments captured, memories rare.
The past entwines with the present's glow,
In every shadow, sweet stories flow.

Ancient echoes, soft and kind,
Within these walls, what truths unwind?
Time's embrace in every sigh,
A timeless charm that won't say goodbye.

The Allure of Purposeful Design

Lines that converge, a vision's grace,
Purpose and beauty in their place.
Each angle sharp, each curve divine,
In crafted forms, aspirations shine.

Thought woven deep, with care it bounds,
Innovation sings in vibrant sounds.
A harmony where function meets,
In every detail, a world repeats.

A Bouquet of Minute Wonders

Petals unfurl, so delicate,
Nature's whispers, we celebrate.
In tiny blooms, vast tales reside,
A bouquet holds a universe wide.

Colors collide in joyful array,
A fleeting beauty, here to stay.
In each small wonder, life can spark,
A tribute bright, against the dark.

An Ode to Refined Crafting

In hands that mold the clay so fine,
Every curve and angle, a design.
With patience carved through sweat and tears,
The masterpiece evolves through years.

Each tool a voice, each stroke a song,
In quiet labor, we belong.
Craft your dreams with fervent heart,
For in each work, we play our part.

The Silken Path of Artistry

Through threads of gold, the visions weave,
A tapestry that helps us believe.
With every stitch, a story told,
In colors bright and shades of bold.

The needle dances, guiding grace,
In fabric realms, we find our place.
Each pattern laid, a journey shared,
In silken paths, our souls are bared.

The Heartbeat of Well-Crafted Sentiments

Words like whispers, softly spun,
In fleeting moments, hearts are won.
Letters crafted with tender care,
Each sentiment a truth laid bare.

In verses we find solace deep,
The echoes of our dreams we keep.
Through ink and paper, love takes flight,
With every line, we spark the light.

Embracing the Harmony Within Us

In quietude, the spirit hums,
A melody of peace that comes.
With open hearts, we join the tune,
Under the watchful eye of the moon.

Together we dance, souls entwined,
In perfect sync, our fates aligned.
Embracing all the light and dark,
In harmony, we leave our mark.

Tailored Reveries

In dreams we weave the patterns bright,
A tapestry of hopes in flight.
Each thought a stitch, so finely drawn,
In twilight's glow, a new day dawns.

With whispers soft, the night recedes,
Through quiet paths, our spirit leads.
Beneath the stars, where shadows play,
We find our voice, we shape our way.

Essence of the Exquisite

A fragrance lingers, sweet and pure,
In moments brief, the heart finds cure.
Each glance a spark, ignites the air,
An invitation to the rare.

In delicate touch, we find delight,
The colors vibrant, bold and bright.
With every breath, a heartbeat sings,
In the essence, love takes wings.

Tapestry of Timelessness

In threads of time, we intertwine,
Our stories told, both yours and mine.
Each moment stitched, with care we hold,
A legacy in colors bold.

Upon the loom, we spin our fate,
In patterns rich, we celebrate.
With every weave, the past unfolds,
A future bright, with dreams untold.

Harmonies Woven in Time

In echoes soft, the past resounds,
With melodies that know no bounds.
Each note a bridge, from here to there,
A song of life, a breath of air.

As seasons change, the chords will shift,
In harmony, we find our gift.
With every heartbeat, every rhyme,
Our souls unite, in woven time.

Ethereal Craft of Nature's Touch

In whispers soft, the breezes hum,
Tender leaves dance, as shadows come.
Each petal's grace, a world unfolds,
In colors bright, the beauty holds.

Mountains rise with timeless might,
Streams weave glimmers in fading light.
Nature's brush paints skies anew,
In every hue, a dream breaks through.

Luminous Patterns in a Silent Room

Shadows play on walls so bare,
Whispers linger in the air.
Light cascades through the window's seam,
Crafting patterns like a dream.

Stillness wraps the soul with grace,
In quiet corners, time finds space.
Each moment glows with gentle thought,
In vibrant stillness, peace is sought.

The Balance of Simplicity and Depth

In golden fields where silence dwells,
A gentle breeze, a story tells.
The simple joys, a quiet bliss,
In breaths of air, we find our kiss.

Depth resides in fleeting time,
A hidden heart, a mountain's climb.
Life's complexities, like shadows cast,
Reveal the beauty in the vast.

Refined Verses in Gentle Echoes

In every word, a whisper sings,
A tapestry of thought unfolds.
Echoes linger, soft and pure,
In the silence, hearts endure.

Gentle rhythms, like a stream,
Flow through thoughts and shape a dream.
Refined verses crafted with care,
Immutable truths weave through the air.

The Alchemy of Shape and Form

In shadows cast, the shapes do play,
Whispers of light in soft array.
Curves and angles dance in time,
A silent rhythm, pure and prime.

From clay to stone, the sculptor's hand,
Molds the dreams in shifting sand.
Each form a story, rich and bold,
In every contour, tales unfold.

Colors blend in muted grace,
Transforming nothing into space.
A fluid stroke, a perfect line,
The alchemy of art divine.

Here in the silence, visions bloom,
Within the heart, dispelling gloom.
In every shape, a soul takes flight,
The dance of form, forever bright.

Symphony in Quiet Hues

A canvas bathed in whispered tones,
Where softest light and shadow moans.
Each brushstroke sings a gentle plea,
Melodies in muted harmony.

The lilac skies and emerald leaves,
In subtle tones, the heart believes.
A symphony of color's breath,
In quietude, it conquers death.

The gentle sway of curtains drawn,
As dawn awakens to the morn.
Each hue, a note in nature's song,
In every space, where dreams belong.

In silence deep, the colors blend,
A tranquil peace, as moments spend.
The symphony of life's embrace,
In quiet hues, we find our place.

Ephemeral Masterpieces

In fleeting time, the beauty lies,
A dance of moments, soft and shy.
The morning dew, the sunset flame,
Each breath a spark, a whispered name.

A sculpture made of drifting sand,
With each wave's touch, it slips from hand.
Moments captured, held so near,
Yet like the wind, they disappear.

A fragile bloom on petals soft,
Its colors bright, its fragrance waft.
Each masterpiece, a glance, a sigh,
In life's sweet pulse, we learn to fly.

In the stillness, we need not chase,
The art of now, our sacred space.
For in the fleeting, beauty stays,
In every heartbeat, in every gaze.

The Artistry of Everyday

A kettle's whistle fills the air,
Hot steam curls up without a care.
The morning toast, a crusty slice,
In simple acts, we find our spice.

The shuffle of feet on wooden floors,
The echoing sound of open doors.
In laughter shared, in tears we shed,
Life's artistry in moments fed.

The sun that rises, softly beams,
In daily tasks, we chase our dreams.
A brush with dawn, a sip of tea,
In every gesture, art is free.

The beauty found in mundane things,
Is where the heart's true language sings.
In artistry of simple days,
We carve our paths in wondrous ways.

The Allure of Precision

In lines exact, the vision grows,
Every angle, a story flows.
A measured touch, a steady hand,
In careful craft, we understand.

Each detail sings, a subtle grace,
Crafted whispers in a race.
With focus sharp, the colors blend,
A symphony that won't just end.

Through perfect forms, the heart takes flight,
In balanced shapes, we find the light.
The allure lies in every seam,
Where dreams awaken, and shadows gleam.

To capture time in strokes so fine,
Where art and heart in union twine.
A mastery that all can see,
In every line, eternity.

Brushstrokes of Diligence

With every stroke, a journey's spun,
The brush reveals what's left undone.
In tenacity, the colors shout,
A labor of love, devoid of doubt.

A steady grip, the canvas wide,
Each mark reflects the heart inside.
From patience blooms a vivid hue,
A masterpiece born of toil true.

Colors dance in rhythmic flow,
Underneath the artist's glow.
Through challenges, the spirit thrives,
In brushstrokes, the passion survives.

Each layer tells a tale of fight,
Resilience born from endless night.
In diligence, the truth will gleam,
Creating worlds from fervent dreams.

Elegy for a Masterpiece

Upon the wall, a story told,
In fading hues, the memories unfold.
A canvas once alive with flair,
Now whispers softly, in silent air.

The hands that crafted, now at rest,
In strokes of genius, they were blessed.
Yet time, a thief, has claimed its toll,
Leaving behind a fractured whole.

In reverence, we stand and gaze,
At splendor lost in time's cruel haze.
An elegy for what once was bright,
Now shadows linger, veiling light.

Yet in our hearts, the art remains,
A spirit bound in joy and pains.
For every masterpiece we mourn,
A legacy, forever born.

A Canvas of Graceful Intent

Beneath the brush, intentions bloom,
A canvas stirs, dispelling gloom.
With every twirl, the colors rise,
Creating dreams beneath the skies.

Soft whispers of a tranquil mind,
In every stroke, new worlds we find.
Graceful arcs and gentle sways,
Illuminate the quiet days.

The palette sings in hues so bold,
Stories of life begin to unfold.
With every touch, a dance of time,
In art's embrace, we climb and climb.

A canvas holds a sacred space,
Where hearts collide and know their place.
In graceful intent, we seek and find,
The art of living, intertwined.

Harmonies of Design

In whispers of lines and forms,
Nature's beauty softly warms.
Colors blend and gently dance,
Creating art, a sweet romance.

Patterns rise and fall like tide,
In every curve, the dreams reside.
A canvas clear, a vision bright,
Crafted with love, pure delight.

Moments captured in still repose,
Harmony in every pose.
Design unfolds in tender grace,
An echo of the heart's embrace.

With every stroke, a tale to tell,
In perfect notes, we weave our spell.
A symphony of sight and sound,
In this design, true joy is found.

Silhouette of Subtle Splendor

In twilight's glow, the shadows play,
Soft silhouettes drift, then sway.
A hint of gold, a whispering breeze,
The world unfolds with gentle ease.

Infinite shapes in evening light,
Dancing softly, out of sight.
Whispers of elegance and grace,
In subtle forms, tranquility's face.

Darkness cradles the hues so bright,
Painting dreams in the velvet night.
Each line a story, each curve a song,
In this splendor, we all belong.

Moments flicker, then softly fade,
In the silhouettes, our dreams are laid.
Nature's canvas, tranquil and wide,
In every shadow, beauty resides.

Curated Moments of Delight

In fleeting seconds, memories bloom,
Curated spaces, the heart's perfume.
A gentle laugh, a tender glance,
Each moment crafted, a timeless chance.

Collections of joy, in frames we hold,
The warmth of a story, forever told.
Embracing time with open arms,
In every detail, life charms.

A sip of tea, a soft embrace,
In curated moments, we find our place.
Fleeting as clouds, yet rich in hue,
Each cherished instant feels anew.

Together we weave, with threads so fine,
A tapestry of laughter, love, and time.
In every heartbeat, a world ignites,
Curated moments, pure delights.

A Tapestry of Graceful Motions

Windswept fields and flowing streams,
Nature dances with vibrant dreams.
Every leaf a story sown,
In graceful motions, life is grown.

Oceans swell with fluid grace,
Rhythms echo, a soft embrace.
With every wave, a whisper flows,
A tapestry where beauty grows.

Stars above in silent flight,
Woven threads of day and night.
In all we see, the dance persists,
An art of life, in every twist.

As shadows shift and time unfolds,
Each movement tells what heart beholds.
In grace, we find the joy we seek,
A tapestry that speaks in soft mystique.

Threads of Love and Imagination

In the loom of dreams, we weave,
Threads of hope interlaced,
Colors bright, softly deceive,
In life's fabric, love embraced.

Whispers dance on a gentle breeze,
Carrying warmth, sweet and pure,
In the heart, a symphony frees,
Imagining joys that endure.

Through the tapestry, stories flow,
Each stitch a moment, a sigh,
A soft glow in the afterglow,
Where hearts find their reason to fly.

Together we craft a grand design,
In shadows and light, we roam,
With every thread, our spirits align,
In this endless fabric, we call home.

The Lilt of Soft Curves

In the moonlight, shadows play,
Curves that sway, gentle and slow,
A rhythm found in night's ballet,
As whispers trace where lovers go.

Time drapes softly on each line,
Embracing forms with tender grace,
In every twist, our hearts entwine,
As laughter glows on every face.

The world softens, hues fall shy,
Underneath the velvet sky,
In the lilt of moments rare,
We find a dance that leads us there.

Holding close what night bestows,
In the charm of curves that tease,
We lose ourselves in warm repose,
Where love's soft lilts bring sweet ease.

Velvet Whispers of Creation

In the hush of dawn, dreams wake,
Velvet whispers float in air,
Colors blend with every shake,
Painting skies, both bright and rare.

Nature's breath, a soft caress,
Gentle hands that mold and shape,
In each heartbeat, we confess,
Life's wild dance, a vibrant drape.

From the canvas, art takes flight,
With every brushstroke, we explore,
Creation's love, pure and bright,
As hope ignites, we yearn for more.

Through the velvet, stories bloom,
In every corner, life replays,
In these whispers, banish gloom,
And let our spirits weave their rays.

A Palette of Elegant Pleasantries

In colors vivid, joy spills forth,
A palette rich, of sweet delight,
Each hue a smile, a spark of worth,
In the dance of day and night.

Gentle strokes of fate align,
Crafted moments, fresh and bright,
In laughter's glow, our souls entwine,
Creating art in pure delight.

From twilight's blush to dawn's embrace,
We paint our dreams with open hearts,
In every glance, in every space,
A tapestry where love imparts.

With elegant pleasantries we share,
The beauty found in simple ways,
In this palette, life's vivid air,
We celebrate our sweetest days.

Curated Moments

In whispers soft, the moments bloom,
Each glance a spark, dispelling gloom.
A treasure found in fleeting frames,
We hold the light, we know the names.

With laughter shared, the time we steal,
A dance of hearts, a sacred reel.
In quiet spaces, memories weave,
The beauty lies in what we believe.

Through golden hours, our stories flow,
In every breath, a chance to grow.
Curated dreams, we dare to chase,
In this embrace, we find our place.

Life paints with strokes of joy and pain,
In every loss, there's room to gain.
Each moment cherished, a precious gem,
In hearts we carry, forever them.

Embracing Subtle Brilliance

In silence found, a spark ignites,
A glow within the coldest nights.
Subtle hints of light unfold,
Whispers of warmth in shades of gold.

Like dew upon the morning grass,
Each drop reflects the moments pass.
In quiet corners, truth reveals,
The heart of life, the soul it heals.

Embrace the glow, the gentle grace,
In every line, the beauty's face.
In shadows cast, the light will shine,
A masterpiece, both yours and mine.

For brilliance lies in tender care,
The little things we pause to share.
In every breath, a chance to see,
The subtle art of being free.

The Sculptor's Serenade

With hands of grace, the sculptor molds,
In silent whispers, the story unfolds.
Chiseled dreams from stone so pure,
In every curve, an art secure.

The chisel strikes with rhythmic sound,
In every mark, the past is found.
Each piece he forms, a breath of life,
A dance of passion, joy, and strife.

In shadows deep, the light will play,
As clay transforms in bright array.
A serenade of form and space,
The heartbeat echoes in this place.

The sculptor sees what others miss,
In every flaw, he finds a kiss.
His heart, a sanctuary of art,
In every piece, a living part.

Hues of Sophistication

In shades of dusk, the colors blend,
A gentle touch, a timeless trend.
Soft pastels and deeper hues,
Sophistic dreams in vibrant views.

With every stroke, a story told,
In rich tones that never grow old.
The canvas breathes, alive with grace,
A dance of colors in endless space.

From twilight skies to morning light,
Each hue reflects the joy of night.
In every palette, whispers gleam,
Inviting all to chase the dream.

Art speaks in tongues both bold and soft,
In hues that lift our hearts aloft.
Sophistication flows like wine,
A journey where our souls align.

Mosaic of Inspiration

Pieces of color blend and sway,
Fragments of dreams in bright display.
Each shard a story, a fleeting glance,
In this mosaic, we find our chance.

Moments captured in vibrant hue,
Crafted with care, each one true.
A canvas alive, a tapestry spun,
In this artistry, my heart has won.

Dreams interwoven, a dance of light,
Guiding my soul through the endless night.
A puzzle of hope crafted in time,
In every corner, a whisper, a rhyme.

Inspirations Born from Detail

In the smallest things, stories unfold,
Whispers of beauty in textures bold.
The grain of the wood, the thread of the seam,
In every detail, a glimmer, a dream.

Petals unfurling, a soft-spoken truth,
Dewdrops like diamonds, the essence of youth.
In shadows that linger, the light finds a way,
To elevate moments in everyday play.

A stitch in the fabric, a line in the verse,
Details remind us of life's subtle curse.
Through the lens of the small, inspiration flows,
In the heart of the detail, true beauty grows.

The Harmony of Form

Geometry dances, a delicate line,
Shapes intertwine with rhythm divine.
Circles and angles, in perfect accord,
Each form a note, a silent chord.

In every structure, a song takes flight,
A balance of forces, dark and light.
Symmetry's embrace in the stillness resides,
In the harmony of form, true beauty abides.

Lines chase each other in waltzes so grand,
Creating a world, a vision unplanned.
In the folds of design, a peace we discover,
The harmony of form, connecting each other.

Gilded Whimsy

In a garden where fantasies bloom,
Joyful colors chase away gloom.
Fairies and dreams in sunlight play,
Gilded whimsy lights up the day.

With laughter that sparkles like stars in the night,
Each moment a treasure, a pure delight.
Imagination dances on the breeze,
In this gilded world, my spirit feels free.

Whispers of magic, soft and kind,
In the corners of corners, wonder we find.
With every heartbeat, the story unfolds,
In gilded whimsy, pure joy beholds.

The Essence of Delicate Craftsmanship

In shadows dance the skilled hands,
Whispering grace in silent lands.
Textures weave with stories told,
Each piece a warmth against the cold.

The finest lines, a gentle trace,
Embrace the heart in crafted space.
With every cut, with every seam,
Reality meets an artist's dream.

Colors blend like dusk and dawn,
A symphony of light is drawn.
Through every flaw, a beauty shines,
In careful work, pure love aligns.

A legacy in wood and clay,
Where hands meet heart in grand ballet.
Each whisper of a chisel's kiss,
Holds tightly to the world of bliss.

Fragments of Aesthetic Reverie

A canvas whispers soft and low,
In colors bright, emotions flow.
Fragments dance in gentle hues,
Whirling dreams in whispered clues.

Each stroke a secret, softly spun,
Tales of moonlight, love, and sun.
Patterns swirl like autumn leaves,
Inviting hearts, the mind believes.

Through windows wide the visions play,
Reflecting night, embracing day.
In every piece, a chorus sings,
Of life and hope and fleeting things.

Collecting fragments, souls entwined,
In every shape, a truth defined.
An artist's heart laid bare and free,
In fragments found, our reverie.

The Poetry of Thoughtful Creation

In quiet moments, ideas bloom,
From shadows deep, they find their room.
Hands craft the words that softly sway,
In written form, they dance and play.

A thought becomes a gentle stream,
Each line a thread, each verse a dream.
With earnest gaze, intentions flow,
Creating worlds we yearn to know.

In echoes of the heart's own call,
We gather thoughts, we rise, we fall.
An artwork forged with care and grace,
In every word, our hopes embrace.

The poetry of life unfolds,
In silent whispers, truth beholds.
With each creation, we take flight,
An endless journey towards the light.

Bells of Elegance in the Calm

In twilight hours, the bells resound,
With elegance in each soft bound.
They chime a tune, so clear and bright,
A tranquil song that warms the night.

As whispers dance upon the breeze,
The world finds peace, the heart at ease.
Each note a sigh, a gentle prayer,
Where time stands still, and souls lay bare.

In quietude, the echoes bloom,
A symphony dispels the gloom.
With every strike, a moment shared,
In rhythm pure, our spirits bared.

Bells of elegance, softly sway,
Inviting hearts to pause and stay.
In every ring, serenity,
A call to see our unity.

Layers of Grace in a Whisper

In morning light, a soft embrace,
The gentle touch, a sacred space.
With every breath, a silent prayer,
Layers of grace float in the air.

A whisper deep, the heart's caress,
In shadows cast, a lightless dress.
Each moment held, a fleeting trace,
Unseen layers, time's gentle pace.

In frail petals, the world's refrain,
Beauty lies in joy and pain.
The strength to rise, to bear the weight,
In whispers sweet, we cultivate.

Hold close the dawn, let worries fade,
In layers found, our souls displayed.
With every dawn, a chance to grow,
Layers of grace, forever flow.

The Dance of Intricate Patterns

In twilight's glow, the shadows weave,
A dance of threads that gently leave.
Each step resounds in silent song,
Patterns form where we belong.

The wind does twirl, the leaves in flight,
A ballet bright, both day and night.
Each turn and sway, a tale unfolds,
In intricate patterns, life beholds.

The moon ascends, a guiding glow,
In every heart, the rhythms flow.
Together bound, by fate's embrace,
We find our dance, our sacred space.

Each moment shared, each echo found,
In life's embrace, we spin around.
The dance we know, forever flows,
In intricate patterns, love still grows.

Threads of Grace in Everyday Life

In morning's light, the simple task,
A gentle smile, no need to ask.
Threads of grace in laughter shared,
In everyday, we show we cared.

The simmering pot, the warmth of home,
In every heart, the love will roam.
A helping hand, a kind remark,
In threads of grace, we leave a spark.

Through crowded streets, in hurried paces,
We find the soul in strangers' faces.
A fleeting glance, a moment's strife,
Threads of grace bring meaning to life.

In quiet moments, we draw near,
In simple acts, love will appear.
Each thread we weave, in joy or strife,
Grace sustains and shapes our life.

Sculpting Stories from Silence

In quietude, the stories grow,
Whispers of dreams that softly flow.
With every pause, the world takes breath,
Sculpting stories, life from death.

The stillness speaks, a canvas vast,
In shades and hues, our shadows cast.
Each tale unveiled in silence's grace,
Sculpting stories in time and space.

The echoes claim, the heart's intent,
In gentle folds, the messages sent.
Sculpting moments, rich and deep,
In silence held, our secrets keep.

So let us dream where silence dwells,
In every heart, a story tells.
We shape our lives, with care and time,
Sculpting stories, both yours and mine.

The Art of Sophisticated Simplicity

In quiet corners, beauty breathes,
Where minimal meets the heart's desires.
A single line draws the gaze with ease,
Whispers of elegance, quiet fires.

Each space is filled with thoughtful grace,
Moments suspended in gentle light.
In the mundane, find a sacred place,
A dance of shadows, a soft delight.

Colors blend in subtle harmony,
Textures speak in whispers of the past.
In every detail, a symphony,
Crafted with care, meant to last.

Through less, we find more, a secret art,
Simplicity's pulse, a soothing balm.
In the stillness, let your spirit start,
Embracing the peace, a tranquil calm.

A Crescendo of Graceful Lines

Feathers touch the canvas of the sky,
With every stroke, a story unfolds.
Curves and angles rise, daring to fly,
Echoes of beauty in tales retold.

Waves of rhythm dance beneath the sun,
Each line flows like a river, unbound.
In the movement, we find we're as one,
A melody crafted in motion found.

Every contour breathes life into the space,
Figures entwined, a beautiful embrace.
In the artwork, we trace every trace,
Each gentle curve, a soft, lingering grace.

As harmonies mingle, visions unite,
A crescendo builds, soaring to the peak.
With every breath, ignite the night,
In graceful lines, the silent speak.

The Veil of Timeless Technique

Beneath a shroud of ancient wisdom's veil,
Crafted hands weave stories of the past.
With patience, a timeless truth set sail,
In skilled precision, a legacy cast.

The brush caresses as it breathes its art,
Each stroke a journey to places unknown.
In the fabric, every thread plays its part,
A tapestry woven, the heart's own tone.

Echoes of masters linger in the air,
Their spirits whisper in each beaten line.
With reverence, we honor those who dare,
To push the limits, to redefine.

Technique stands strong as time moves ahead,
In the crafted, the soul's essence gleams.
As shadows dance where artisans once tread,
We find ourselves in the silence of dreams.

The Silence of Crafted Dreams

In the hush of night, dreams take their flight,
Whispers of hope tread softly on the ground.
Each thought a spark, ignited by the light,
In the silence, lost wishes abound.

Crafted with care, our visions collide,
Gentle echoes of what we hold dear.
In stillness, the heart's secrets reside,
Patience reveals all that we fear.

Artistry blooms from the depths of the mind,
Every creation, a tale to be told.
In the quiet, seek moments that bind,
Memories held in the hands of the bold.

As we wander through shadows of the night,
Let the silence cradle each crafted dream.
In the darkness, find your inner light,
And weave your hopes into the unseen stream.

Elegance Woven Through Time

In whispers of silk, the past unfolds,
Threads of history, each tale retold.
Glimmers of grace in every fine seam,
A tapestry woven from dreams that gleam.

Seasons have passed, yet beauty remains,
Captured in patterns, love's sweet refrains.
Echoes of elegance, soft as the night,
Dancing like shadows, a delicate light.

Through ages we wander, hand in hand,
In the fabric of life, we ever stand.
Moments embroidered with laughter and tears,
A journey of elegance, spanning years.

With each careful stitch, a story to share,
The essence of time woven with care.
In the quiet of dusk, where memories play,
Elegance whispers, guiding our way.

Traces of a Gentle Touch

Fingers that linger on soft, warm skin,
An imprint of love that runs deep within.
Gentle caresses that soothe and renew,
In the silence, the heart speaks true.

Moments like petals fall softly to earth,
Each touch a reminder of love's great worth.
In a world that spins wildly, we find our peace,
In traces of touch, all worries cease.

Time may grow weary, yet we remain close,
In gestures of kindness, our souls compose.
A dance in the twilight, a sigh in the air,
Traces of a gentle touch, beyond compare.

In solitude's embrace, soft echoes call,
Reminders of warmth that encapsulate all.
With love's tender whispers, we learn to believe,
Traces of a gentle touch never leave.

Reflections in Silken Waves

Glimmers of light upon the sea's embrace,
In silken waves, we find a sacred space.
Ripples of time, a soft lullaby's song,
In nature's mirror, where hearts belong.

The ocean's depth holds secrets untold,
Whispers of dreams, both new and old.
Cradled by currents, we drift and sway,
Reflections in silken waves, guiding our way.

With each ebb and flow, we dance with the tide,
In harmony's rhythm, our souls coincide.
Together we wander, like shadows at dusk,
In the world of the waves, there's beauty and trust.

The moonlight bathes us with silver and gold,
Stories of ages in the waters unfold.
In this gentle embrace, we find our reprieve,
Reflections in silken waves, we believe.

The Language of Fine Details

In whispers of ink, the story begins,
Each word a treasure, where beauty spins.
A flicker of grace in the space where we write,
The language of details, pure and bright.

Brushstrokes of passion, a canvas alive,
Every nuance captured, where art will thrive.
The rhythm of heartbeats in delicate lines,
In the dance of creation, our soul shines.

Moments enshrined in the softest embrace,
In the quiet of thought, we find our place.
Crafted with love, each detail a part,
The language of fine details speaks to the heart.

From shadows to light, every curve tells a tale,
In the world of the fine, our spirits set sail.
With patience and care, we cultivate dreams,
The language of fine details, woven in seams.

Delicate Layers of Thought

In quiet corners, whispers grow,
Soft echoes of dreams we sow.
A tapestry of wonder spins,
In fragile shells, the journey begins.

Each layer unfolds truth anew,
Ideas dance in morning dew.
A gentle breeze, a silent muse,
In gentle thoughts, our fate we choose.

Beneath the surface, treasures lie,
Waiting for the bold to try.
Delicate layers, rich and deep,
In every heart, a secret we keep.

Beauty Sculpted by Intent

In hands of grace, the clay is shaped,
Visions born, passion draped.
With every stroke, a story made,
Beauty blooms where dreams invade.

Intentions pure as morning light,
Ignite the world, set wrongs to right.
From heart to earth, the art will flow,
In glowing cast, our spirits glow.

Molding moments, time stands still,
Each crafted line reflects our will.
With purpose clear, we chisel fate,
A masterpiece, we cultivate.

The Harmony of Intent and Creation

In rhythms soft, both heart and hand,
Together weave the life we planned.
Intentions strong, yet gentle too,
In every note, our truth shines through.

Creation sings in silent sounds,
Where nature whispers, freedom bounds.
A symphony of earth and sky,
In harmony, our spirits fly.

Through light and shadow, paths entwine,
With grace we tread on sacred line.
Each creation spark, a flame of thought,
In unity, the beauty caught.

Shades of Grace Against Time's Canvas

On canvas rich, the shades unfold,
Stories wrapped in hues of gold.
With strokes of love, we paint the day,
In gentle grace, we find our way.

Against the ticking clock we stand,
With visions bright, we shape the land.
Each moment pass, a brush in hand,
Marking time with dreams so grand.

In every hue, a memory wakes,
Through trials faced, our spirit aches.
Yet in the blend, we find our place,
Embracing all, the shades of grace.

Inheritance of Timeless Beauty

In the garden blooms, secrets unfold,
Petals whisper stories, young yet old.
Beneath the sun's gaze, colors reside,
In every blossom, memories abide.

Through gentle breezes, voices emerge,
Echoing love in a silent surge.
Graceful like daisies, wild yet free,
A testament to all that we see.

Threads of Serenity

In the stillness, the heart finds peace,
Soft whispers of nature never cease.
Woven with care, each moment shared,
A tapestry rich, lovingly prepared.

Gentle streams flow, caressing the land,
Each ripple a promise, softly planned.
Under wide skies, time drifts by slow,
In threads of serenity, we grow.

Sculpted Dreams in Soft Shadows

In twilight's embrace, dreams take their flight,
Soft shadows dance in the fading light.
Carved by moonbeams, a vision so clear,
Echoes of hope in the evening sphere.

With each soft breath, we mold our fate,
In sculpted forms, love will await.
As dawn breaks softly, we'll find our way,
In dreams of stillness, forever stay.

The Elegance of Every Stitch

In the fabric's weave, stories entwine,
Every thread whispers, creating design.
Hands skilled and tender, with purpose they guide,
The elegance shines, in each careful stride.

Through colors and patterns, our lives reflect,
The beauty of moments that we collect.
A legacy spun in love's gentle light,
In the elegance of every stitch, we write.

The Grace of Form and Function

In curves that dance, in lines that flow,
A silent story, a visual glow.
The art of purpose, a beauty supreme,
Where function whispers, and shadows dream.

Crafted with love, in balance so true,
Each piece a marvel, in shades of hue.
The elegance speaks in subtle delight,
A harmony found in day and in night.

From shape to form, from thought to stage,
Designs unfold like a turning page.
In the hands of makers, with passion ignited,
The grace of creation, forever invited.

In unity born, in freedom expressed,
The blend of art leaves hearts truly blessed.
Form and function in a dance of the free,
An everlasting ode, for all to see.

Essence of Artistry in Movement

In every motion, a tale unfolds,
A symphony written, as life beholds.
With rhythm and grace, we glide through the air,
Capturing moments, beyond compare.

The dancer's spirit, alive with the beat,
Footsteps resonate, like hearts that meet.
Canvas of life, in colors so bold,
The essence of artistry, a story retold.

Spinning and twirling, we chase the light,
Each fleeting gesture, a beautiful sight.
Transcending the limits of earth and of sky,
In motion we flow, like a wind's gentle sigh.

In harmony woven, our bodies align,
The melody lingers, the stars intertwine.
Artistry breathes in each step and each leap,
In the dance of existence, our spirits keep.

The Whimsy of Fine Creations

In a world of wonder, where dreams collide,
A spark of whimsy, a playful guide.
Crafted with glee, each piece tells a tale,
Of laughter and joy, where spirits set sail.

Colors that sing, in patterns they play,
Dancing off edges, in a bright new ballet.
Sculpted with care, with a wink and a grin,
The magic of creation, where stories begin.

From knick-knacks of charm to fine works of art,
Each creation a journey, a piece of the heart.
Whimsical echoes in every fine detail,
Spreading enchantment like a sweet summer gale.

The beauty of play, in each twist and turn,
Inviting the world to laugh and to learn.
In fancy and fun, our spirits set free,
The whimsy of fine creations, a legacy.

The Palette of Momentary Elegance

With every stroke, a memory made,
A fleeting whisper, in colors that fade.
The canvas awaits, a breath of the now,
An echo of beauty, a gentle vow.

Brushes dance lightly, in hues soft and bright,
Capturing shadows that merge with the light.
Each moment cherished, on canvases spun,
The palette of life, until day is done.

Ephemeral sparkles, in twilight they gleam,
Colors enraptured in a painter's dream.
In the whispers of time, we find our embrace,
Momentary elegance, a timeless grace.

As seasons do change, and memories bloom,
We find elegance finds a way to consume.
In the fragility of time, we're fully alive,
The palette of elegance, where dreams thrive.

Intricacies of Design

In shadows play the lines we trace,
With curves that soar, an artful grace.
Each thread a story, colors blend,
In patterns forged that never end.

Symmetry in chaos found,
A dance of shapes that do abound.
From chaos springs the calm so near,
A tapestry that draws us here.

Through every fold, a world unfolds,
The whispers of the brave and bold.
In each creation's breath, we see,
The spirit of humanity.

With every stitch, a life embraces,
In woven hearts, the love it chases.
Design entwined with dreams so grand,
A journey set by skilled hands.

A Symphony in Stitches

Threads of gold and silver shine,
Creating harmony, so divine.
Each loop a note in rhythmic play,
A canvas where our dreams can sway.

Beneath the fingers, fabric sings,
In softest whispers, joy it brings.
Patterns emerge like melodies,
In every stitch, our hearts at ease.

The needle dances, graceful, light,
Composing tales through day and night.
With vibrant hues, our stories weave,
A symphony that we believe.

In swirls and knots, our spirits rise,
An orchestra beneath the skies.
Through artful hands, our visions blend,
In stitches, love will never end.

The Dance of Delicate Hands

With gentle touch, the fabric glides,
In rhythmic movements, beauty hides.
Each fold a step, each seam a turn,
In this dance, our passions burn.

Fingers trace the patterns' grace,
In every stitch, we find our place.
As yarn entwines, the stories grow,
A tale of warmth that we bestow.

The art of weaving life's embrace,
A tender touch, a soft embrace.
Like dancers on a vibrant stage,
We paint the world, our hearts engage.

In every knot, a promise sewn,
Delicate hands, in love, have grown.
With every thread, our dreams expand,
United now, by delicate hands.

Patterns of Poetic Beauty

In every weave, a story lies,
Patterns whisper, never die.
Each thread connects, a gentle bind,
In hues of heart that love defined.

A tapestry of life unfolds,
In colors bright and whispers bold.
Threads of hope and dreams we share,
In crafted forms, we show we care.

Through intricate designs we find,
The beauty held in every mind.
A glimpse of joy and sorrow's tune,
In stitched reflections of the moon.

The artistry of love displayed,
In patterns rich, our hearts conveyed.
Together we create and see,
The poetry in our tapestry.

Milton Keynes UK
Ingram Content Group UK Ltd.
UKHW020937041024
449263UK00011B/566